7 STEPS TO SHARK TANK

A FIRST-HAND ACCOUNT OF A SHARK TANK JOURNEY BY AN ENTREPRENEUR WHO HOOKED A DEAL!

BY: **NATE** SALES & CUSTOMER SERVICE EXPERT
HOLZAPFEL

Shark Tank **Rules and Tiers**

Preface

Daymond John has stated that it's easier to get into Harvard than on *Shark Tank*. In 2014, 40,000 people applied, fewer than 100 got to pitch to the Sharks, and even fewer made it to air. Out of that number, only a scarce few make a deal on air, and after some due diligence over the next few weeks, the Sharks have a chance to decide if the deal was represented properly. If it was, then you are in business. I was one of those people.

Lots of people have questions about *Shark Tank*—so many that it became obvious that I should organize my experience so people can learn from my it.

THOU SHALT ASK GREAT QUESTIONS.

This is not a pith guide or a how to get on *Shark Tank* instruction manual. It's a timeline of what I went through and how long it took. I cannot speak to everyone's experience; I know a lot of people who have been on the show, and we all share similar experiences. That being said, I do not speak for anyone but myself.

This is not intended to be a "tell all" or a "*Shark Tank* Secrets Revealed" document. It is merely an inside look at the process I underwent. I love *Shark Tank*, ABC, CNBC, Sony Motion Pictures, Finamax llc, the producers and staff of these organizations, and of course, the Sharks. I have nothing negative to say about any of them, and if I did, I still probably wouldn't tell anyone.

My goal is for people who are interested in behind the scenes from a contestant's perspective to enjoy the show more and appreciate how hard everyone works to make this show a possibility.

If you follow any of my work on social media, YouTube, or my writings with the *Huffington Post*, you may be familiar with my Ten Commandments of Selling:

Commandment One. THOU SHALT HUSTLE.
Commandment Two. THOU SHALT LOVE THY CUSTOMER AS THYSELF.
Commandment Three. THOU SHALT STRATEGIZE.
Commandment Four. THOU SHALT CREATE VALUE.
Commandment Five. THOU SHALT LISTEN.
Commandment Six. THOU SHALT BE THYSELF.
Commandment Seven. THOU SHALT RUTHLESSLY ELIMINATE DISTRACTIONS.
Commandment Eight. THOU SHALT ASK GREAT QUESTIONS.
Commandment Nine. THOU SHALT BE CREATIVE.
Commandment Ten. THOU SHALT KEEP IT SIMPLE.

You can get a complimentary copy of my Ten Commandments on my website. www.NateHolzapfel.com. I apply these commandments in my business, and you will see them interspersed throughout this document.

THOU SHALT KEEP IT SIMPLE.

Shark Tank changed my life. I would do anything for anyone on the show or anyone who broadcasts it. The moment I aired on that show was a pivotal moment for me.

We sold ONE MILLION DOLLARS of our product when we aired on the show, which created capital that we would use we to build Mission Belt Co. and springboard us into what it is today—not to mention my personal career as a customer service/sales customer engagement specialist speaker, trainer, and consultant has escalated since I aired on this show. If Columbus remembered finding land or Neil Armstrong landing on the moon, they would probably tell you that that was the moment when it all changed.

Most everyone who had dealt with me before *Shark Tank* knew I was great at my job, but not util 8,000,000 people saw me all at once did my acclaim as a salesperson become clear.

THOU SHALT LOVE THY CUSTOMER AS THYSELF.

The number one question everyone asks me is, "Was it was worth it?" My answer is YES, without a doubt. I love *Shark Tank* and had an amazing time going through the process. It was life changing for me in so many ways. Life is full of opportunities, most of which we must create on our own. If you are thinking about applying for the show or have been contacted by a producer, consider the possible opportunities. Most people see *Shark Tank* as a way to get money; it certainly is that, but it's so much more. For the people who know what to look for and how to get it, this opportunity can literally change everything for you.

People will tell you that there are no shortcuts in life. While this may be true most of the time, there are certainly faster routes available for those prepared to risk it. *Shark Tank* was one of these for me.

While my intentions in writing this are to convey some interesting information about *Shark Tank*, it is also my hope that you will read this and see how much *Shark Tank* applies to everyday life and business. Wherever we go, we are selling. Whether it is our products or our abilities, we are always looking for that next opportunity that will move our career and life along. For those who are willing, *Shark Tank* can certainly be this. For those who are not looking for *Shark Tank*, this can still be beneficial.

THOU SHALT CREATE VALUE.

I have so many great stories and experiences that have come from my involvement with the show and the Sharks, specifically my favorite, Daymond John. This account of my experiences is honest and from my heart. I have learned that with an experienced guide, or in this case, someone who has traveled the road you are considering, you will have a sincere advantage—the educated and trained version of you as opposed to the uneducated and the untrained version of you. I personally like to get the inside track. I wanted to compile all the details I wish I had known prior to applying to the show and definitely prior to airing.

The most important thing to remember about *Shark Tank* is it is seldom about the product. The Sharks know all the new products on the market, and they know instantly what is going to be big and what is not. Also, they know that they really won't have the hands-on time to work and develop a marketing plan for the product. This should come as no surprise to most as they are all millionaires and billionaires with their own successful businesses to run. No, the product is not what they are examining. They are examining the person.

Re-watch a couple of episodes on *Shark Tank*. Notice it is often the pitcher, not the product, that makes the difference. The Sharks want to work with someone who is going to go the distance. They want someone they believe can sell and someone who is confident enough to be successful.

I write this not to discourage anyone or to boast, but to shift your perspective about the show and how to prepare for it. Don't think about your product as much while you're reading this. Instead, think about yourself, what you are good at, and how you will transfer that onto the camera. It is important to never try to be someone you are not.

The Sharks can smell a fake from a mile away and will rip you apart instead.

THOU SHALT BE THYSELF.

Go in the Tank with confidence and control. Know your product and all the numbers of your business, and it will pay off.

I am a believer in the hustle. Hustle is more than just doing something or working hard at it; it's the symphony of the mind, body, spirit, and soul, all working in harmony to achieve the goal or task at hand. In fact, it's my first commandment of selling, Hustle is the grit that it takes to make something happen. Hustle is the next step beyond. It is acting on that idea. Look at *Shark Tank* itself. Are you guaranteed that you will be given a deal? No. Are you guaranteed that you will even get on the show? Absolutely not. But if you don't try, you will always have a giant "what if" floating around for the rest of your life.

THOU SHALT HUSTLE.

Far better for you to try and fail than to never know. At least this was my mindset at the time, and it remains so. Just before I applied, I told a few people that I was thinking about doing it. All three told me that I shouldn't spend too much time on it because it probably wouldn't happen. These were people who counseled me, loved me, and wanted what was best for me.

I don't want to get to far off topic, but I can assure you that most advice you will receive in life from friends and family will be conservative and cautious. This is understandable. While there are many true stories of disaster and failure, its important to realize that every huge success you will ever hear about throws caution to the wind.

In retrospect, its almost funny that I was counseled to not even try or not put too much time into it. If I really think about it though, it strikes me as a real personal accomplishment to push through the haze of doubters, trusted relationships, and naysayers and pursue my own path to where I am today and where I will be in the future.

It would have been easy to have heeded the words of wise men and advisors who counseled me against it. The road to success has not been clear nor has it been easy, but it certainly has been worth it. So go on and try! Nothing bad can come from trying. As my mother always said, it never hurts to ask.

THOU SHALT ASK GREAT QUESTIONS.

Some of us fear rejection. The truth is all of us fear it, but some of us, so very few of us, have the courage to stand up to rejection and recognize that without rejection, there is no acceptance, there is no glory, and there is no better way to find out what you are made of. In fact, it's the only way.

We all have something to offer. Each one of us has a story to share, and some of these stories, ongoing as they may be, have resonance. As you fail, your story gets longer and in many cases better. Think about all the movies and books we all love. No one wants to hear a story about someone whose life is perfect and all goes as planned. Actually, the opposite is true. *Robinson Crusoe, Gladiator, Top Gun*, the *Little Mermaid, Star Wars*, and even the *Little Engine That Could* all faced obstacles, leading up to the finale, the grand success.

THOU SHALT CREATE VALUE.

Don't forget the first rule of *Shark Tank*:

Rule 1: This is TV.

This is a living, breathing show that makes money by creating television so compelling that advertisers and networks will expend millions of dollars a minute to be able to advertise during the commercial breaks. So the first rule is to remember, you must be part of an engaging show. This is not only about great ideas or great people. This is about everything all at once.

Being nice isn't enough. In fact, we have all seen some real stinkers on the show that no one likes, but guess what? They are engaging. Do you or your pitch help create engaging TV? That's a question I want everyone to think about, not so they can second guess themselves, but so that they can improve their pitch and their story as needed. This is not to say lie or even change details, but you have to make it exciting to watch. Is there a party in you that no one has ever unlocked? This may be the time to do it. Remember throughout this guide, only the most engaging TV moments will record and possibly air.

Make sure that you are smiling and that you are ready to answer questions. Presentation is everything. It's interesting to know that a great product is not enough. You have to offer something worth filming. It costs millions of dollars to produce an episode of *Shark Tank*. Are you worth filming? Do you know your math? Are you interesting? Are you going to create exciting moments for viewers by being yourself and being truthful?

One of my favorite moments on *Shark Tank* was when Dallas Robinson from Kiss Stix got Barbara Corcoran and Kevin O'Leary to kiss on air. That was both brilliant and compelling. I think everyone watching that night realized how crazy that was. It meant something. It was different. Dallas is a great entrepreneur and is really smart, but it was his engaging pitch that got him air time on the most popular prime time show on Friday nights.

THOU SHALT BE CREATIVE.

I present the *Shark Tank* experience in seven tiers, as follows:

Tier 1 Applying to *Shark Tank*

Tier 2 Practicing the Pitch

Tier 3 Getting a Call Back

Tier 4 Working with the Producers

Tier 5 Receiving the Invitation

Tier 6 Pitching and Filming your Product/Service

Tier 7 Airing your Segment

Tier 1 Applying to *Shark Tank*

There are three ways to get on *Shark Tank*:

(1) *Live Casting Calls*. The most common and the most obvious is live casting calls. This is an open call announced on *Shark Tank's* official site and social media., Occasionally some of the staff that support the show and the casting directors post to their social media.

This one is the easiest because it puts you in front of decision makers immediately. You line up for a number, then as a group you wait till they call your number. Then you are expected to pitch. You only have a few seconds to make a case for yourself, even if you are there for 2-3 minutes.

Producers and casting people are on hand to see what you are made of. It's pretty intense, but it's a great way for them to see you in real life. Most people have a hard time getting their point and what they have to offer communicated via the written word, so this is really a great way to have a dialogue as opposed to a one-and- done email.

When you address the casting crew on site, you will often be at a public place, sometimes a campus, or occasionally a gymnasium or ballroom. You will need to be prepared for what to expect. There will be no professional lighting; they may film you with a simple camcorder and take notes with a pen and paper. This throws a lot of people off as they expect a more official setting. It's really quite unimpressive in that sense. Be ready to pitch at a moment's notice the second you hit the parking lot.

Once you are ready to pitch at the drop of a hat, you are ready for the second rule of *Shark Tank*.

Rule 2: Everyone is important.

Treat everyone like they are Mark Burnett himself. Recognize that there is no way to tell who is who from just looking at them. People are often surprised how young everyone seems. The truth is that TV is a young person's business. Most of the staff are under thirty, and you will discover that they are all on similar career paths to become producers, directors, and other leadership roles within production. These people do not aspire to get on the other end of the camera; they like it where they are and recognize the potential longevity of production vs being the one filmed is far greater. These are incredibly smart, organized people who have gotten this job through sheer hustle, sweat, and hard work. These positions are highly coveted, and you need to respect them accordingly.

Personally, I treat everyone well. I still have the names of the people who shuttled me and met me at the gates, and I have since thanked them all personally. I take great care to love everyone. Once again, we can put a spin on my second commandment of selling. After all, isn't that what this is? Selling ourselves? Creating a narrative that will allow us to tell our story and hopefully land a Shark! Commandment #2. *Thou shalt love thy customer as thyself.* Let's love everyone if we are going to be successful. If we are always truly selling ourselves, we need to realize that everyone is our customer, our critic, our audience. Make sure that you have the proper respect for everyone on set. These people work 12-18 hour days to make these shows come together in a timely, meaningful, and yes, engaging way.

THOU SHALT LOVE THY CUSTOMER AS THYSELF.

As you begin your pitch, remember engagement counts. Take yourself up a few notches from where you would normally speak or present. Take the time to be engaging. I train people from all over the country on how to pitch and present well. It's amazing how few people learn how to accurately project themselves and who they are. We are all different, but many times the real you is lost in translation, and only a part of who you are comes through.

THOU SHALT BE THYSELF.

I certainly have met people who are better diluted since no one could stand a 100% dosage of their personality. But for the most part, people worldwide have something to share, especially Americans. I don't say this because I am one, and I know how big *Shark Tank* is in Canada, but the truth is most people on the show are American. The reason for this is because Americans are crazy. There's not a Canadian that the world that would disagree with that statement! Remember, it's about engagement!!! Be sure to be alive, or at least act like it for the few minutes you are there. You can get back to being quiet and reserved as soon as you are out of the building.

This show is not for the faint of heart. It is potentially disastrous. Most people experience a lot of criticism on air, but the good news is that the casting crew will not beat you up. They are loving people with nothing but the best intentions for you and your product. After you meet with them for a few minutes, you will be told that they will let you know if they are interested. It's a "don't call us we'll call you" policy. As you can imagine, 40 thousand people apply for this show every year, and only serious candidates can expect callbacks. The good thing about in person is that it's a chance for you to put flesh and blood and the best version of you right in front of them. Live castings are a great way to get on *Shark Tank*.

(2) *Producers contact you*. This is the second most common way to get on *Shark Tank*. It happens all the time, but there is little you can do about getting noticed. If someone from casting sees you on FB or at a trade show or meets you, you could end up with a shot, but it doesn't mean that you will be selected to film or even air. Lots of people don't make it through the seven tiers. In fact, most don't. Fewer than one percent of all applicants end up on TV, and even fewer get a deal.

If you have been contacted by a producer, the biggest pitfall is to think you are special or that you don't have to do anything else because "they want you." They have merely asked you for your number; you still have to "date" and hit it off if you want to hear wedding bells. Overconfidence is so common in this particular case.

I think that people with inflated egos will sometimes be brought onto *Shark Tank* just to be brought down to size. This is not to say that they are bad businessmen or women or that they don't deserve a shot, but they are hampered by their egos. Be humble. Every time you pitch is an opportunity to learn about your presentation skills and what it is about your product that resonates with your potential customers.

The same rules hold true for the live casting calls. Be your best version of you, take it up two notches, and be engaging.

Rule 3: Never assume you will get on the show.

It's so imperative that you keep your head on your shoulders. The dating analogy is pretty indicative of how you have to approach this. They are looking for engaging TV; the perfect product will not be enough. The producers are feeding the Sharks deals. They want the people that air to get deals. Imagine a show where they just let anyone on. You'd watch hundreds of episodes with no deals being made. Then the show would be off the air. (Remember the first rule of *Shark Tank*.)

If you don't seem like you can present well or make a good partner for the show, they will look over you to find the people that have a real chance at this life-changing opportunity. Remember, the producers of this show genuinely want to help people. Many have stayed in touch with me and are always cheering me on. Be the candidate who will allow them to put you in the Tank!

(3) *Send an email.* To this day, I'm the only person I know who has gotten on the show through an email. I'm sure many have; I just don't know any. Put it in perspective. I know about 20 people who have aired on the show, and while some may come to me before they apply and air, few contact me later to tell me about their experiences. They are so caught up in their own little worlds that they forget there is much to be learned from someone who not only aired on the show, but also made a deal, and whose company generated one million dollars in sales in the first three weeks after airing.

If there are no nearby casting calls, I encourage you to follow my lead. Email is harder because it doesn't allow you to stand out as much, but there are ways, and the way I did it obviously worked really well. It was a short email—short and sweet. It included a picture of myself and it was very clear about who I was and what I hoped for. A copy of this email is included in my Five Secrets of Selling training course.

This email changed my life. A few days after sending it, I quit my job and started selling the belts door to door. Three days later, a call came, area code 310, Culver City. I didn't answer it as I was with my most recent belt converts/customers. When I listened to the voice mail, I shouted out loud a huge "yes!" I was ecstatic. I called my brother and told him that they had actually contacted us back and wanted to talk! It was a big moment. Little did I know that was only the second tier in my *Shark Tank* experience.

When I called back the number, a soft-spoken man answered and introduced himself. He went on to explain to me that it was not his decision who went on the show, but it was his job to suggest who might be good. He asked a few questions about my email and informed me mine really stood out. He said if the producers were interested, they would call me; if not, they wouldn't.
This is the fourth rule of *Shark Tank*:

Rule 4: Don't call us; we'll call you.

This is possibly the most memorable of all rules. It's a constant series of events that leave you speechless and irresolute. And so, I waited...

Don't bother the people that contact you. I never once called and asked for an update. They are super busy and really don't have time to be bothered. In fact, if you are bothering them, you may be saying goodbye to any chance that you might have had. Use this time to continue to practice. This way you are always ready to go and make the most out of any moment that could come your way.

Tier 2 Practicing the Pitch

This best way to prepare for this is to pitch your product to anyone and everyone. You love your product more than anyone else? Show it. A problem that I have noticed about many entrepreneurs is they are embarrassed to talk about their products or businesses. They will often shortchange many of the details and be afraid to get too passionate and in "sales mode" because they are afraid of being ridiculed or scrutinized. Well, I have news for these hesitant would-be salesmen. No one scrutinizes more than the Sharks, and if they find anything wrong, they will ridicule you until you want to cry. It's a whole lot better to have your Cousin Jerry insult you in private than Kevin O'Leary do it on national TV.

By the time I got into the *Shark Tank*, I had literally pitched mission belts a thousand times. Any opportunity I had I would go into it. "Everyone owns a belt, and many people own a couple, and in thousands of years, this everyday accessory has hardly ever changed..." If I had a belt on me (and I normally did), I would finish the pitch and sell the person the belt right there. You have to be ready.

My advice to anyone who has to do a video pitch is to imagine your customer specifically and pitch to him and him alone. Don't be general; don't try to pitch to everyone. Imagining that you are pitching to one person, your pitch will seem more personal no matter the size of your group, making you much better for TV because all those people at home will be engaged.

Tier 3 Getting a Call Back

For me, the callback and the emotions it evoked have never worn off. I still treasure that moment and place it close to monumentous as marrying my wife, my children being born, and getting my driver's license. It was a huge "top ten" moment for me as far as emotions were concerned. The feeling that I had, what it took to get a call back, and the vindication that it was the right thing to do swarmed with that hot summer day in June, which would ultimately change my life as I knew it.

The truth is that it was just the second step to the holy grail of entrepreneurship. What would come next would prove to be one of the most stressful, emotional, and longest time I have ever held my breath.

Tier 4 Working with the Producers

Two junior producers contacted me a week later. A man and a woman, though I almost feel funny calling them that as they were younger than I was at the time (33), but they were hardly immature. In fact, they were so professional I was surprised when they told me their ages.

They expressed their interest in me and what I was doing. That had a lot of questions for me, things that would come out on air mostly. Why I wanted to be on *Shark Tank*, why they thought I'd be good, and what was important to them, etc. A very nice two-way conversation ensued over the next 30 minutes. They requested that I send them my pitch in video format for them to watch. They emailed me a list of things to cover. At the end of the conversation, they repeated the previous disclaimer, "Don't call us. We'll call you."

At this point, I realized that it would be a lengthy process, but I had no idea how very long it would be before I was on the air, or if I would even have a chance to film!

I set about making my film on a friend's borrowed camcorder as this was still a bit before drop box and before great video could be done on a smartphone. We used a piece of butcher paper and wrote out the points they wanted me to cover. I have never shown that video to anyone but the folks at *Shark Tank*. At some point, I may put it on YouTube or on my website.

The most difficult of this part of the process was that I wasn't speaking directly with my customer. You see, it doesn't matter how many times you have sold your product, your pitch will always be different when you have different customers. It is essential to engage your customers, ask questions, and listen to their responses.

THOU SHALT LISTEN.

I was instructed to ramble and not edit or cut it because they wanted to see that I could talk for 5-8 minutes uninterrupted. Those who know me or have seen me in in action realize that I can talk for hours on end with no pauses or breaks. But they didn't have a clue of what kind of crazy they were dealing with at that point. Soon they would find out.

The producers returned my call, and I was in the fourth tier of the process. They loved my video and had lots of great things to say. Of course, this was all before they asked me to make it 1.5 minutes long. At this point, they laid out some expectations as far as timelines and general processes. It was at this point that they told me that if I could work with them over the next few (6) weeks. I would then potentially be flown to LA to meet, practice, and then do a dry run for the final decision makers. Then, if all went well, I would be given a chance to film. Now that doesn't mean I would air. Many people who film do not air.

This fourth tier brought on paperwork like you have never seen. Disclaimers, agreements, appendix after appendix, line after line. These agreements are similar to what you would expect in a small phone book as far as length and sheer girth. It took days to go through filling out, filling out, filling out and filling out more. Back and forth as we rushed to meet the terms.

In the days prior to Mark Cuban's addition, *Shark Tank* and its affiliates could take ownership in your company at their discretion. This "discretion" normally came out to around 2.5% to 5%, obviously not a massive amount, but enough to make an impact. This meant that many small business owners before me lost equity in their company for only a chance at getting on *Shark Tank*.

Mark Cuban stopped this. He felt that startups need all the help that they can get, and he did not want to see too many people losing their bread before they even had a chance to win it.

The paperwork was the dreariest task I had undertaken in some time. This is coming from a guy who once dug holes for a living. Trust me, it was tedious. Every other page needed to be signed sometimes in two or three places. Disclosures of equity. Background checks for everyone, info from your intellectual property attorney, trademarks, etc. were all thoroughly researched.

The attorney for the show, who shall remain nameless along with the rest of the staff and crew, was helpful and concise. He was perhaps the pickiest of all I encountered on the set, but definitely one of the most appreciated as he was all business and helped me get done all that I needed to get done.

Meanwhile, I was on the phone with junior producers off and on, practicing my pitch and keeping it down to under 1.5 minutes. They would listen, make some suggestions, and then send me back to the drawing board. As I have repeatedly said, before this I had pitched my product hundreds of times, but nothing could have prepared me for this. They refined my sales skills, and because of their inside knowledge about the Sharks and their personalities, they were able to help me prepare to better know my audience and better sell to them.

This was a fun time, and as the weeks went on, I felt more and more assured about my chances even though they constantly assured me that there was no guarantee of anything. We were communicating by phone and email throughout this process.

Tier 5 Receiving the Invitation

Finally, one day they called and said: "Nate, would you like to come to LA?" "Boy, would I!" was my response if memory serves correctly. Once again, this moment, though not a definition of success, was overwhelming. Remember that this was still no guarantee that I would even film, let alone air or make a deal with a Shark! They told me that I would need to come in three days, and that they would send the ticket to me. I was, however, responsible to ship my products and anything I wanted on set.

At this point, I didn't have a proper point of sale because up until this, I had only ever been in stores that had their own belt displays. In fact, all I had were three colors of belts: brown, a couple of white, lots of black, a few prototypes that ended up gracing the stage with me, and the belt that I was wearing, which is on display in the back of my closet next to my lederhosen. While this was great for my business overhead, it also meant that up until this point, I never needed a belt rack, which would in fact be essential for my presentation to the Sharks.

If there was anything that I could have known beforehand, it would have been this. You might not need it if you get on, but I had to scramble, and it was a close call. To the reader who makes it this far in the *Shark Tank* tiers, make sure you have everything ready. Setting out immediately, I did my best to find a rack for my presentation. If you watch my episode (Season 4, Episode 22), you will see a very generic chrome-plated belt rack that I found in LA on the internet.

Because there was not sufficient time to have it shipped to my home and assembled, I had to ship it to the stage in LA and assemble it there. I do not hesitate to say that this was perhaps one of the scariest moments for me. I literally never saw the rack until the day I was to present.

I was instructed to tell no one that I was going to come down to LA to film for *Shark Tank*. Earlier I had received little blurbs about this. Conversations would often end with something like "and as a remainder, please don't tell anyone that we had this discussion." But before LA, this request came more as a commandment than anything else with how sternly they presented it.

Tier 6 Pitching and Filming your Product/Service

Three days later, I was collected at LAX and loaded up with a few others who seemed to be there for the same reason, though I didn't know for sure because we were asked not to talk to each other about our businesses.

We loaded a van and were driven to a hotel, where we were given a per diem for food. I'm told now that *Shark Tank* will actually pay you a very minimum wage for being on TV; it's almost nothing from what I have seen. I was given $80 and a room key. It is so low because of the opportunities that the show opens up to you. It's true that it was only $80, but I ended up getting 50,000 dollars for my company.

After I had gone up to my room and unpacked, I called my junior producers, and they told me to be in the lobby at 5:00 am and asked me what I would be wearing.

They told me that I should wear a suit and tie to the presentation, but I politely asked if I could wear my jeans, Vans sneakers, and a blue button up shirt, from which I removed the label. (No brands or logos other than my own were permitted.) You can actually see the black stain form the permanent pen ink I used to blot out the logo label of my shirt, which ended up getting cut off anyway.

The producers really pushed me for the suit and tie, but I told them that I did not want to segment my market by making people feel like it could only be worn to a formal occasion. By dressing down, I made it seem like a casual accessory, but during the presentation, I was able to make the point that it could be worn to formal events with no trouble.

After I was settled, I set out to sell some Mission Belts. I got a cardboard box from the front desk and went out on the street and started going door to door. I had not intended to make that part of the show. I was just doing what I had been doing.

A new place meant new customers, and I took advantage of it. Later, Mark Cuban would go on to tell the world how much he loved my work ethic and said that he could relate to this because he used to go door to door as well. Going door to door ended up being the best thing I did during my stay in LA—with the exception of showing up.
The next morning came early. I have never been an early riser. Having fallen asleep around 12:30 PST or 1:30 am MST, which I was used to, I woke up the next day, threw on my clothes, and went down to the lobby, where I waited for one hour for the shuttle. *Shark Tank* does a great job of making sure that potential contestants do the waiting, not them, which is really smart based on the costs of doing business and the time of the

Sharks being so limited. I can't tell you how awesome it was to have everyone in the show call you an entrepreneur. To me there is no greater title.

We loaded a bus and had a short ride to Sony Motion Pictures, where we unloaded and walked around for a few seconds, just long enough to get a chance to see some of the studio grounds. We then filed in to a huge empty stage. It was across from where they filmed Jeopardy and originally the Wizard of Oz. This was a truly amazing place to be and in its own way, magical.

We sat in metal chairs on the bare floor while a man stood up and introduced himself as the producer of the show. He then congratulated us on making it this far, but cautioned us with yet another disclaimer that we might not even be filmed. He then told us that we would all pitch to him and his staff and then go back to our hotel, and that later that night, they would tell us if we would be invited to film.

The room was anything but intimate; it was a completely empty sound stage, with the exception of 70 people, 10 long folding tables, and a dozen *Shark Tank* hopefuls. They called us up one by one. When it was my turn, I got up and started to speak, and the whole place went quit. Everyone's eyes were on me. For a moment, I felt as if my fly were down. But right when the thought came, I kicked into gear. All my practicing and years of salesmanship came back, and I was flying. In the end, I felt great about what had happened, but once again, "Don't call us, we'll call you" was the message. We were dispatched to our hotels.

Later that night, I got a call from my junior producers, informing me that I would in fact be getting filmed! They once again gave that great disclaimer, however slightly updated, "You will film, but there's no guarantee it will air." I was given a similar instruction as the night before. "Be downstairs at 5:00 A.M. or bust." I wouldn't, however, film till two days later. That left a whole day to myself. Fortunately, my brother had driven down to

LA the day before, and we spent time going over my pitch together and mostly discussing what we would be willing to do if we were offered a deal.

The next day, I woke up and hurried down the elevator, I was down at five, and this time I only waited a few minutes. I do believe that they would have done absolutely nothing had I missed the shuttle. There is just no time to make emergency plans for people who fall off the program.

We were then taken to a small building that had half a dozen dressing rooms and were shown to rooms that had our names on them, two sets of people to each. I was to appear on the show by myself, and was assigned with some guys who had a neat outdoor product. We sat there not knowing what to say, but of course we began to talk. Twenty minutes later, both of them were proud new owners of Mission Belts, and I had a cash padding in my back pockets. Several entrepreneurs that season can be seen wearing Mission Belts on stage. What can I say; it's what I do. I'm a salesman.

One by one, over the course of the day, entrepreneurs were taken out, gone for two hours, then back, hurried away by a staffer, and then put in a van and returned to a hotel.

I was the last to pitch out of 12 that day. This is arguably the worst time to pitch. Everyone, including the Sharks, is tired from a long day of filming. They start filming at the same time as we did. Unfortunately, for me they are not like normal TV personalities. They don't need money or the show, which means that they don't have to act at all, so fatigue, hunger, and boredom can play a big part in their decision making.

At about 4:45, I was escorted out of the dressing room. I had been to makeup six hours earlier to take the shine off of my face, which was now drenched with perspiration. It was September 26th, and LA was on fire. It must have been over a hundred degrees, and the AC offered little relief. My producers had been in and out all day, mostly ferrying people back and forth. I was taken to a stage where I could hear the Sharks talking, I was told to be quiet and was then moved to an area only defined by the black curtain that hung all the way from the 30-foot ceiling to the floor. There was a construction-type light metal chair and a fan that was on full blast.

In the show, the Tank is a beautiful room that looks like it belongs in a gala, but everything around that room was pretty sketchy. I was half expecting someone to come in and shoot me full of crack cocaine, and then be physically assaulted by middle aged men from Eastern Europe in exchange for money. It was easily the most unpleasant place that anyone could possibly devise within the walls of that studio.

I sat there for almost an hour. Then I was told it was my turn. They walked me around the back of the set. I could see the lights and cameras of the set. They had precariously put a mic on me while in the "room of fan," and several men approached from behind the doors. One asked me how I felt, another touched up my face with powder, and yet another stood on a ladder and held the ropes on pulleys that would open the iconic doors to the formidable *Shark Tank*.

As the doors opened, I walked out of them down the hall with a sense of purpose. I cannot tell you how surreal it was to finally be there, to have earned my place in front of the Sharks. I had been instructed to stand on the piece of tape on the Turkish-styled rug that graces the set. Up close, that rug is really quite disgusting. It's marked up, stained, and looks like someone or something had been dying on it for the last year. After you walk onto the carpet, you are told that you will need to wait for 1 to 1.5 minutes while they check lighting and sound. It is actually quite anti-climactic because after what you feel is your best power walk into the room, you just stand there awkwardly, waiting to start and not being allowed to talk.

It was at this time I remembered all the documents I had previously signed, allowing *Shark Tank* to use my image as they saw fit. I decided then and there that I was not going to have any dumb looks, so I locked eyes with Mark Cuban. I didn't smile or frown. I was emotionless. I locked eyes with Daymond next, then blearily and so on for four to five seconds each. On my first pass, Mark looked at me and smiled. Then Daymond gave me a bit of a scowl, probably wondering what was wrong with me. Then, he squinted his eyes and looked at me. Lori smiled and almost waved with her brown eyes, and then Robert smiled.

After Robert, I went back to Lori and did about five passes. By my third pass, O'Leary had his hand up to his eyes, looking at his red wristband watch, Daymond was looking up in the air over my head, and Cuban's smile had turned to a glare. Then the director said "Go" –not action or a countdown, simply "Go," and I transformed from cold stare to biggest smile you have ever seen, "Hey Sharks!" Every person in the chairs sat up straight. I had taken control of the room. The space was mine to keep or lose.

I would recommend that you stop reading for a moment and watch my pitch on *Shark Tank*. It's available on iTunes, Season 4 Episode 22. Its only $1.99 per episode, and I get exactly $0 every time someone downloads it, but it will give you perspective and complete the story. Watch it. Then, resume your reading here. If you feel you can't wait, by all means, read on.

The pitch went great. I got a few laughs as I made a self-deprecating joke about my weight. Then the questions. These pitches go on for about an hour. You have to remember that only a small percentage of the discussion makes it to TV—if it makes it at all.

Rule 5: Don't look dumb, ever.

The opportunity to look dumb is enormous. It's not easy going an hour with people who are experts at finding holes in your business, grilling you all at once. It takes perfect posture, something I often discuss in my sales and pitching trainings; there is a physical posture and a social posture that can make or break us.

When an entrepreneur walks down the hall with the aquariums, he/she walks out to an oriental rug of sorts. This rug looks as if it had served as the floor of a surgery ward in the Civil War. It has stains on it, many of which are unclear in origin. It is covered in tape, residues, and what I assume is human sweat. After all, it's *Shark Tank*, and they smell fear. If Mark Burnett called me and asked me to store that rug at my house, I would rent another house to live in while it was there. The camera may add 20 pounds, but it removes stains better than any cleaning product ever.

After you reach the rug of chum, you are then asked to stand there for one whole minute while they adjust lighting and sound, so the moment is awkward to say the least. Remember cameras are rolling, and thanks to the phonebook-sized waiver you filled out, they can use that awkward time and cut and paste it anywhere they like. I don't know if this is done, but I wasn't about to risk it. I decided a better strategy was needed.

THOU SHALT STRATEGIZE.

I locked eyes starting with Mark Cuban for three seconds each, emotionless, not upset or happy, not nervous or confident, just an intense eye-to-eye stare. No smiles, no frowns. I went on to Daymond, O'Leary, Lori, and finally, Robert. Then back again in reverse. Each pass became more and more awkward for the Sharks. On the first pass, Cuban smiled at me and even gave me an acknowledging raise of the head; Daymond looked at me like I was mentally unstable. (he's from NY); O'Leary stared back at me, squinting a little with the same emotionless stare that I was wearing myself; Lori smiled politely as did Robert. By the fourth pass, O'Leary was looking down at his watch,

Daymond was looking at the ceiling, and Mark was looking at me, probably wondering what was wrong with me.

Then it happened. The director said "Go." And I went from emotionless to all smiles, all expressions I could muster, eyebrows raised, teeth in full smile formation, and I said "Hey Sharks!" everyone smiled as they jumped back an inch. I had given them something they hadn't seen before. It was posture at its finest. Many people ask what was the trick to not getting beaten up in the Tank, it had a lot to do with posture.

Rule 5: Know your numbers.

Obviously knowing my numbers, the sixth rule of *Shark Tank* helps, but first impressions and presentation are everything. This set the stage for what would come. Once again if you are interested in sales theory and pitch creation, read my Five Sales Secrets, but its almost impossible to tell the story without a little sales acumen here and there.

You will notice that Lori actually politely bowed out. Instead of frowning or saying boohoo, I thanked her for her opinion, and went on to the next Shark, almost dismissing her. This was necessary to retain control of a room that could become entirely hostile in a flash. Lori was very kind to me. All were and are nice. I got a big hug form her the other day when I saw her in LA. I love Lori.

I love all the Sharks, I respect them all immensely, and none of my tactics that I employed should be considered a reflection on any of them. I was simply doing what I do best. Selling. If they weren't making an offer, they were not going to be part of the discussion, period.

THOU SHALT RUTHLESSLY ELIMINATE DISTRACTIONS.

Sharks and investors respect control and will respect you if you can walk the fine line of negotiations, and they do not want to do business with someone acting like a jerk or being weak or needy. This is all part of posture. I won't get into the anatomy of a sale. If you are interested in that, you can download my "Five Secrets to Selling" program. This account is to talk about what to expect when and if you apply for *Shark Tank* and are lucky. I have always been lucky.

After I made my deal with Daymond, I walked off the stage and was de mic-ed and congratulated by all the crew. My junior producers were jumping up and down. I knew at that moment my life would never be the same. They told me not to tell anyone—not even the other entrepreneurs—about what had happened one way or the other.

I went back to my assigned dressing room, and one of Daymond's employees came in and talked to me for a few minutes, smoked a cigarette, then said we'd be in touch.

Then three other groups of entrepreneurs and I piled into a van. One group was disgruntled, and all they kept saying is how they couldn't wait to get out of this stupid town, etc.; the other people were quiet. I had a smile on my face as big as the van we were riding in; it was obvious to all who had gotten what they wanted and who didn't.

Instead of being taken back to the hotel, I was in previously, I was taken to a much nicer five-star hotel, where I was given a beautiful room. The van took the disgruntled group to the airport as I think they had demanded it, though I can't be sure. They were pretty upset. Later, I watched them on the show. They had gotten a deal, but one partner didn't like the deal apparently. I'm sure the Shark they worked with negotiated something. The Sharks are great people and want what's best for everyone (in my experience).

I called my brother and our other partner Jeff, and we couldn't have been happier about the deal we had all made. It was a surreal moment. Everything I had been working on for the last three months was finally a reality, but there was still no guarantee it would air.

Tier 7   Airing the Segment

There was no way to know when or if it would air. In LA, I had been told so many times that it might not, that I half expected it not to. Eight months later, we find ourselves on the TV guide, three whole days before *Shark Tank* called us to let us know we'd be airing. It read, "Man with new type of belt" as one of the five entrepreneurs.

When *Shark Tank* called, we were told that we still might not air. A national emergency , a major hurricane, a political assassination, or war could derail scheduled TV programing for weeks. Anything was possible. The main concern is that an entrepreneur will spend lots of money and time for the show to air, upping inventory and servers etc., and then not having it air, and then being liable for the extra expenses.

The night of the show, I got a call from a NY number that I had never taken a call from. I had talked to Daymond a lot through his office numbers etc., but this number was new. It was Daymond, and he told me to sit back enjoy and have fun with it no matter what happened. Twenty minutes later, I remember looking at my phone and seeing the email inbox go from 3 to 99+ right before my eyes. It had started on the East Coast. Later, I would recognize this as a pivotal moment in our business, the tipping point. We had sold over 600k in the months leading up to this day. We ended up selling $186,000 that first night. The next day was a similar number. The following Monday, one of Daymond's employees, the one I had met on set after the deal was struck, called me to ask how we had done sales wise. When I told him 500k, he literally freaked out. We knew we'd hit a million within a few weeks. Direct and online kept the sales coming in for over a month steadily.

Shark Tank is a surreal experience for anyone who can get on the show. I won't claim credit for the success that I had. It came from a lot of great partners, a supportive family, and at the end of the day, a little bit of luck. For anyone who is thinking about going on the show, I offer three suggestions: (1) Be honest with yourself about your product. A lot of entrepreneurs will put their heart and soul into a product and will quickly turn blind to how much people will actually want it. It's sad, but when it comes to *Shark Tank* or even entrepreneurship in general, don't waste any time on products that aren't going anywhere. Be objective; (2) Once you know that you have a good product, just go for it. Practice your pitch, and know your product; and (3) Know your numbers inside and out. Don't think you know everything and are ready to go. Over preparation is the key. Know all of the numbers that can possible apply to your business. Revenue sales up to that point, cost of manufacturing, margin percentage, what you will do with every penny of the money if they invest in you. Etc. No detail is too minuscule.

They didn't show it, but I was grilled about my business for almost all of my presentation, and from what I understand, that holds true for most people who appear on *Shark Tank*.

One more comment. ..
If you are lucky enough to get on *Shark Tank*, make the most of your experience, and ENJOY.

I hope this helps!
Nate